MW00365510

Cat Tales

by Sara Pitzer

August House / *Little Rock*

P U B L I S H E R S

Printed in the United States of America

10 9 8 7 6 5 4 3 2 1

LIBRARY OF CONGRESS CATALOGING-IN-PUBLICATION DATA
Pitzer, Sara.
Cat tales / by Sara Pitzer.
p.   cm.
ISBN 0-87483-095-8 : $11.95
1. Cats—Anecdotes.   I. Title.
SF445.7.P58   1989
636.8—dc20
89-6807
CIP

First Edition, 1989

Cover illustration by Byron Taylor
Production artwork by Ira Hocut
Typography by Lettergraphics, Memphis, Tennessee
Design direction by Ted Parkhurst
Project direction by Hope Coulter

This book is printed on archival-quality paper which meets the
guidelines for performance and durability of the Committee on
Production Guidelines for Book Longevity of the Council on
Library Resources.

AUGUST HOUSE, INC.   PUBLISHERS   LITTLE ROCK

Acknowledgments

Thanks to the many people, friends, relatives, and strangers, who shared their stories, especially the students in my English 1101 and 1102 classes at the University of North Carolina-Charlotte.

This is for my kids, Lee and Dana, and my husband, Croy,
all of whom have suffered many indignities because of the cats
but love them anyway.

Contents

Introduction

Cats don't invite indifference. You either love them or you hate them. People who love them will tolerate almost any inconvenience for the sake of their cats and other cat people will understand. People who hate cats will go to almost any lengths to avoid them, and all like-minded individuals will understand.

All these stories are from people who love cats, but love them for what they are, not for one myth or another that has been promulgated about them. For instance, Carl Sandburg wrote about fog and silent cat paws; real cat people know that the noise of a couple of cats running across the floor, far from being soft, sounds like somebody let horses loose inside.

Cat people don't want to see you testing the old wives' tale that cats always land on their feet or that they have nine lives or that their whiskers keep them from getting into any space too small to get out of again. Whether such stories are true or not isn't the point. If you love a cat, you know your cat is unique—beyond all generalizations. If you love ten cats, you know each one differs from all the others.

Cats seem as varied as snowflakes; it's hard to imagine that any two could ever be alike. Yet they have commonalities. You'll certainly see your cat reflected in this book, though if a given tale had been about your cat, it would've been a better story, of course. And that's the fun of it—identifying the common traits and appreciating their absolutely individual development in our own pets. That means you can probably read any story in this little book and mentally write another version: how it would have gone if the main character had been your cat.

And as cat people, we all have in common one truly wonderful thing. As long as we have our cats, we'll never be quite as lonely as other people.

A Cat's Name Tells You Something about the Cat and Something about Its Owner

Originally, Squirrel's name was "Cat." That changed when she had to have treatment at the veterinarian's. The receptionist in the office refused to accept her for treatment without a name to put on the form. She didn't think "Cat" was enough of a name. "That's generic, not really a name," the receptionist said.

"But it starts with a capital letter. That means a specific cat, just like 'Mother' with a capital 'M' means a specific mother," Cat's owner said.

"I'm sorry, ma'am, I can't write down 'Cat Dietrick.' It's not sufficient," said the receptionist.

"Okay, okay," Ms. Dietrick said. "Then write down 'Squirrel. Squirrel Dietrick.'"

Since the animal wasn't a squirrel, the receptionist reasoned, Squirrel must be a name, not a generic label. Smiling, she wrote it down. The vet treated the cat, collected a generous fee, and had his receptionist add the registration form to his regular files.

And that's how Cat became Squirrel.

Helen Weil is a Southerner who works in publishing. She acquired her Siamese in downtown Atlanta, saw that the cat was a southern belle, and necessarily named her Melanie, as in *Gone with the Wind.* "Of course, I've been reduced to the role Butterfly McQueen played," Helen said.

Also literary, but more serious, the Parkhurst cat is named Marlow, after the character in Conrad's *Heart of Darkness,* because he was found in an undeniable heart of darkness, the mouth of a dog. The dog picked Marlow from a litter of kittens and carried him home. No one knew where the litter was, so there was no returning the kitten. Marlow got his name and his first feeding from human hands when he was four days old.

The Burnetts favor literary names, too. From James Thurber's *Thirteen Clocks* came Zatch and Guggle. From *My Fair Lady* came Higgins. Then children changed the cat-naming scene in that family, as they change most things in most families. Instead of literary allusions, the new cats were Bumbum, Guyoo, and Dagon, baby talk adaptations of Bumble, Cleo, and Blackie.

Another child, Heather Fleming, reached near-literary quality when she put down the funny papers and named her cat Marmaduke.

A teenager received Euclid from his relieved parents as a reward for pulling a high school geometry grade up from a D to an A. The boy's sister, an English major, tried to make that one literary too, walking around the cat quoting Edna St. Vincent Millay: *Euclid alone has looked upon beauty bare and seen her massive sandal set in sand . . . .* But the boy stopped that. He told his sister his cat didn't have nothing to do with any naked beauty queen that had big feet. Then he threw his basketball right at her stomach and she went away, so Euclid is still just Euclid for passing geometry.

Then we have the gentleman who acquired his cats in pairs and named them accordingly: Rag and

Muffin, Salt and Pepper, Peaches and Cream, Mutt and Jeff, Hi-O and Silver, Simon and Garfunkle. Trouble is, misfortunes over the years broke up the teams, leaving that good man with Rag, Salt, Cream, Mutt, Silver, and Simon, which didn't make any sense at all unless you knew the history.

You knew after you'd listened to him for just a few minutes how Motorboat got his name. When poor Motorboat was gone and a successor came into the house, this family, too, went literary. They call him Ishmael.

Quark belongs to a physicist who really wanted to name his Persian Einstein, but the family had already given that name to a mutt with lots of gray and white curly hair.

And when poor Elsie went to be spayed, the veterinarian checked under the long white fur and suggested neutering would be more appropriate, so Elsie immediately became L.C.

Conversely, George, the Greenhouse Cat, also a long-hair, had won the hearts of countless customers and staff, mostly by sleeping by the cash register and allowing all who paid to pet. When the neutering trip to the vet revealed that George really should have been named Georgette or Georgia or Georgine, Tim Lowder was willing to make the change. He loved the cat but didn't have strong feelings about its name. Not so Tim's customers. It was George they knew, George they expected, and, in the end, George she remained.

Porch Panther, a gray long-hair, lives on the back porch of a house rented by a bunch of college boys. Most of the time he's happy there, sleeping in his square cardboard box, eating from his tin dish, and chasing chipmunks, but occasionally he likes to come in. Then he leaps to the screen on the window and hangs ten until someone lets him in. When they're looking at Porch Panther from that inside angle, the guys call him "Buttercrotch."

When Ann Gaither moved into her new house, it was clean and empty except for a rolled-up carpet the previous occupants had apparently forgotten

when they left. She had her movers carry it out, before they started bringing in her furniture. As soon as they lifted it from the floor, it started to wiggle and hump as though it were alive. They rolled open the rug, which turned out to be a well-worn Persian, and out sprang a blue-eyed white cat that appeared to be part Siamese, and immediately started rubbing back and forth against Ann's ankles. She got rid of the Persian but kept the Siamese, who simply had to be named Cleopatra.

The Pitzer family has always relied on generic names because they've indulged in such quantities of cats that they can't think up original names fast enough. In the beginning was Gray Kitty. And then Little Gray, followed by Little Gray's Little Gray. The next gray cat was simply "Stray."

She was followed by the black-and-white Dempsey, found at a dumpster. When Dempsey disappeared, only to be succeeded by another black-and-white look-alike, the Pitzers figured that if Sly Stallone could go all the way to Rocky IV, they could go at least to Dempsey Two.

Fluffy Cat, Fat Boy, and Tiger got named the usual way, just describing how they looked. Then, when another gray cat showed up, there didn't seem to be much left to call her except Orphan Annie. Everyone agrees, the next kitten to wander in will be "Selah."

Sometimes things aren't all that obvious. A person could spend a lot of time wondering how cats got named Nacotia, Lowatha, and Keema, or Tootsie Roll, Pretzels, and Pony. It's true that all these names have been taken, but since they don't carry specific stories, you probably could borrow one if you get desperate.

Cats Are Loyal

Edward was a British tax collector in Ethiopia. From the time the Persian was a kitten, Edward was devoted to Bombay (named for the gin, of course), playing with her every evening without fail. They had one game. Edward rolled a large ball of heavy twine around the house, unraveling it as he pushed it from room to room for Bombay to chase. At the end of the game, Edward rewound the ball of hemp and put it in Bombay's corner, next to her pillow and water bowl.

The time came when Edward had to travel about the country, collecting taxes, and he was away from home for days in a row. Edward's wife, who didn't share his interest in cat games, figured her duties included feeding and watering the cat but definitely stopped short of playing with it.

Gradually, Bombay taught herself to roll the ball of twine from room to room herself, pushing it along the same route Edward always used. Then, probably not wanting to annoy Mrs. Edward, Bombay would retrace her steps, winding up the twine as well as she could, until she had it gathered in its customary spot next to her pillow and water bowl. Without fail, Bombay strung out her twine and then pushed it back to her corner every night until Edward came home again to resume his rightful role in the game.

Ordinarily, Mouser Smith preferred to be outdoors most of the time. He came in to be fed, he tolerated a little petting from the children, and he didn't mind having his picture taken with the presents under the tree around Christmastime; but aside from those concessions, Mouser wanted to be out back in the woods with the chipmunks and squirrels and big bugs. But when the Smith's grade school–aged daughter became ill enough to have to spend several weeks in bed or lying on the couch, Mouser stayed with her almost all the time, sleeping beside her on the bed or stretched across the back of the sofa, within easy petting distance. As soon as the child was well enough to return to school, Mouser went back to the woods.

You will notice, dear reader, how short this chapter is.

Cats Act Like They Have Nine Lives Because They Know You'll Go to Any Lengths to Save Them

No one knew the old house had a walk-in fireplace behind the kitchen until the day the cat fell down the chimney which ran up the inside of the house and had been cut off (but not plugged) back under the eaves of the attic. But Squirrel found it and fell down all three stories to the hearth behind the cupboards on the first floor. Everyone heard Squirrel crying that morning and thought she was inside a cupboard, until removing all the pots and pans revealed no Squirrel. It just *sounded* like that's where she was. Several hours of tracing the cries ended up with the searchers in the attic because there wasn't anyplace else to go. Shining a flashlight down thirty feet to the hearth below, Squirrel's human mommy saw her walking back and forth on the old bricks, with no way to get up or out.

Having to crawl on her belly to get back under the eaves to the chimney complicated rescue efforts.

23

Each trip in and out risked getting 150-year-old splinters in the knees and belly. Plan One involved fashioning a muslin bag around a wire loop to hold the mouth open and attaching it to knotted pieces of bailing twine. When the bag was lowered, Stupid Squirrel wouldn't get in to be pulled up. Plan Two involved using a piece of leftover meatloaf as bait to lure Squirrel into the bag. Stubborn Squirrel didn't like meatloaf any better than anyone else. Plan Five, an open can of tuna fish for bait, almost worked, except that by the time Stuck Squirrel had been raised about fifteen feet, she had eaten all the tuna and jumped out of the rescue bag. A hot dog and some nasty words finally worked on Squirrel. She jumped into the bag to chew on the hot dog, started to jump out again about halfway up, but froze on the spot when her mommy gave up on the nice "here kitty, kitty" noises and said, instead, "Damn it, cat, if you jump out again, I'm coming down there and wring your neck." Sweet Squirrel settled back into the bag and purred for the rest of the ride to the top. And that's how Squirrel got saved by a hot dog. The story made the *Pennsylvania Mirror* newspaper under the headline, "Bagging Squirrel."

This story about a cat rescue made the *Charlotte Observer*. A man tried to rescue a kitten from a pine tree by backing his pick-up against the tree and standing in the truck bed to lasso the top of the tree. He pulled on the rope to bend the top of the tree down to where he could reach the kitten. The rope snapped, the tree straightened with a whoosh, and the kitten was catapulted, spread-eagled, over the roof of the house and into a neighbor's swimming pool. From there the kitten was rescued by a youngster practicing half-gainers.

This one made the media too. Clem was let out one cold, snowy night and disappeared. Eight years later, he sat on the doorstep and cried to be let back in. Nobody knows where he was or who helped him survive, but Clem hasn't gone back outside since.

Tidbit was gray with white trim, a bold, fearless hunter. When he was two he got caught in a double spring trap that had been wired to a fallen tree serving as a natural bridge over the creek. He was trapped, exposed to temperatures fluctuating between zero and five above for four-and-a-half days before the family finally found him. His temperature

was 89° F. A cat's normal temperature is around 101° F. Although he lost most of his hind leg, he was soon hale and hearty again, and back to his old practice of leaping up onto barstools.

Lizzie had a thing about the roof. She climbed a tree and walked across its limb to the roof every day, without ever figuring out how to reverse the process when she wanted to come down. Since the rescue operation involved a stepladder, fishy cat food for bribery, and heavy gloves for protection, everyone agreed it would be a good idea for her to learn to get down by herself. The she'll-come-down-when-she's-hungry theory was abandoned after four days. The let's-teach-her-how-to-climb-down approach was abandoned mid-effort, when the twelve-year-old teacher nearly broke a leg trying to demonstrate how to crawl backwards across a tree limb. A serious plan for leaving her up there with food, water, and a litter box was vetoed one windy afternoon because the house is in tornado country. Ultimately, the best solution seemed to be the first one, with the ladder and bribery. Now, the ladder and gloves are handy just inside the garage door. Lizzie's learned the routine and, while she still expects the fishy bribe each day, doesn't have to be coaxed anymore to come to the edge of the roof. It's about like any other cat household, except that instead of asking if the cat's been let in every evening, they say, "Did you bring Lizzie down?"

When Susan and Lee first got Kipper, they had no children, so, of course, the kitten was their baby. One of Kipper's first moves was to climb a tall pine tree, perch on the lowest limb, which was forty feet off the ground, and cry piteously for rescue. Lee was in good shape, but he knew he couldn't climb forty feet up a limbless tree trunk. While Susan was crying and trying to console poor Kipper from the ground, Lee decided to try to use his crab trap, a boxy thing made of chicken wire, to rescue Kipper. A cork float is attached to the trap by a long piece of rope. Lee's plan was to throw the float over the limb, catch it, and use it to hoist the crab trap up to the level of kitten on the limb.

Lee reasoned that the kitten would crawl onto the top of the crab trap and then he could play out the rope to lower her back to ground gently.

After three hours of throwing, Lee had to quit trying to throw the float over the limb because his arm was too tired to move anymore. While they stood at the foot of the tree, Susan tearfully massaging Lee's shoulder and both of them trying to figure out what to do next, Kipper calmly began to back down the tree. Minutes later she was on the ground, flicking her tail and looking for food.

"What ever made me think she would get onto that trap anyway?" Lee said.

Sheri Hartnett's Muffy jumped unnoticed into the clothes dryer before Sheri finished loading it and closing the door. Sheri started the dryer and went upstairs to do the dishes. Ten minutes or so later, her brother, Billy, got nervous about the bumping-thump noise the dryer seemed to be making with each revolution, went to the basement to see what was making such a racket, and felt around in the clothes inside. He touched something firmer than a towel but almost as limp. Muffy was a mess. Her breathing was labored; her whiskers were crinkled; her fur was singed; the pads on her paws were burnt.

They leapt into the car, Sheri driving because she did not want to be the one holding Muffy if the cat died, and raced at eighty-five miles an hour, running red lights and weaving through traffic, to the animal hospital. The veterinarian packed Muffy in ice, gave her several shots, and kept her at the hospital. A few days later, Muffy was well enough to go home, but it was weeks before her whiskers straightened out, her fur became soft, and her paws healed. Now Muffy not only won't go near the dryer, she's even a little suspicious of anyone wearing clean clothes.

If it hadn't been for "Melancholy Baby," Sammy wouldn't have made it. Ever since the day after the party, everyone had been going around calling, "Sammy, Sammy, here Sammy, Sammy." But no Sammy. He was not the kind of cat, they agreed, to wander off and settle in with the first neighbors to feed him a better grade of chow. In fact, he wasn't even one to wander past the end of the driveway. Something was definitely wrong.

It was almost a week later, and a couple of the teenagers were over from next door making bad jokes about playing "Melancholy Baby," and do you know "Misti," and how about "Mountain Greenery." Obviously these kids were operating on information from old movies on TV; what the kids knew from their own experience was Pink Floyd and Bruce Springsteen, neither likely to play "Melancholy Baby." Given all that, the kids soon decided to have a little contest to see who could actually play "Melancholy Baby," and they clattered down the cellar stairs to the gameroom. Nobody'd been down there since they finished cleaning up the day after the party.

The first tentative chords of "Melancholy Baby" sounded wrong, not only because nobody knew the song, but also because the piano's hammers weren't striking the strings cleanly. The kids opened up the top of the old grand and found Sammy, too weak to cry or do much of anything else except make the piano play funny.

As far as anyone can figure out, Sammy must have smelled an appetizer or a stray potato chip inside the piano sometime after the party and, in the process of going after it, knocked the piano lid down on himself.

Sammy made it, but he's never been quite the same. His vision is impaired. He doesn't think much of music. And he hates parties.

You could hear Muffin's sad little meows all over the house, but no matter how you followed the sound, which clearly came from the study, there was no Muffin. It seemed as though she must be just on the other side of the wall, except that when you went into the next room, the sound still seemed to be coming from just on the other side of the wall. The first good clue came from a sound that seemed to be pages turning or wastepaper being crumpled— something involving paper, anyway. It led them to the bottom desk drawer, where they kept letterhead and envelopes. Pulling open the drawer, they found Muffin, not looking all that miserable, considering, hunched in the back of the drawer behind the envelopes. She must have crawled in and fallen asleep while someone was working at the desk. She didn't realize she was trapped and begin to cry until she woke up sometime after the drawer was closed. Muffin had only torn up two sheets of paper, just enough to attract attention when people stood near the desk calling, "Kitty, kitty."

Ansley Fleming isn't handy and he knows it. It's okay, because generally people don't expect a choir director to be handy. So when Ansley removed a nasty old medicine chest from his bathroom wall, plastered over the hole, and installed a new cabinet perfectly, it was a big deal.

While he was still admiring his handiwork, Ansley started hearing voices out of nowhere. As a choir director, he always thinks he might eventually hear heavenly choruses, but he hadn't supposed that it would happen in the bathroom, nor that the sound would be like a cat's meow.

Ansley has a good ear. The longer he listened, the more certain he became that he was hearing Bertha. Bertha's neither a faithful choir soprano nor a departed distant relative who might be singing in celestial choirs. Bertha is Ansley's cat.

Ansley has a good ear. The longer he listened, the more certain he became that Bertha was singing from inside the bathroom wall.

There was nothing for it but to take down the new medicine cabinet, reopen the hole in the wall, and rescue Bertha. Bertha, of course, is fine. The new medicine chest was never quite right after Ansley put it back, because, although Ansley has a good ear, he just isn't handy.

Penelope's a Siamese that used to live at Magnolia Place, an inn in Savannah, Georgia, when Bonnie was innkeeper. The inn is famous for its butterfly collection, but no one guessed it would be a butterfly that almost did Penelope in. It was a beautiful spring day. Bonnie had opened the door, attached a leash to Penelope's collar, and fastened the leash to a railing on the back stoop so Penelope could enjoy the sweet air. Penelope had a grand time. As people came and went, they watched her eyeballing robins and batting at butterflies. No one saw it happen, but apparently

Penelope got so enthusiastic in her pursuit of butterflies that she threw herself over the edge of the stoop, turning her collar into an all-too-effective noose. At what must have been close to the last possible minute to save her, a maid noticed Penelope dangling, shrieked, and grabbed her up. Bonnie came running to pump Penelope's ribs with her hands and administer a little people-to-cat resuscitation. Penelope revived, washed her face, and went to sleep in the room with the butterfly collection, presumably reasoning that dead butterflies do not present the same hazards as live ones.

Little Billy Frey was only about two and a half years old when his eight-year-old brother brought home two kittens. The kids hid the kittens in the shed for fear they wouldn't be allowed to keep them if their parents knew. Billy gave up his security blanket to make the kitty bed. That was almost twenty years ago. Billy still remembers.

Cats Are Smarter Than Dogs

You can't get six cats to pull a sled.

No cat will keep fetching a ball and returning it to you if all you're going to do is toss it away again.

Your cat won't bark at the UPS man when he's delivering Christmas boxes from your rich aunt, get you fined by nipping at the meter reader, or do something dumb when he realizes that the bookmobile is going to park in front of your house all afternoon.

What self-respecting cat would permit itself to be clipped and groomed like a poodle, with little ruffs around its ankles and all the hair shaved off its body?

A cat refuses to roll over and play dead when she isn't really.

You can't get a cat to stand up and beg for a greasy scrap from your dinner plate. If there's anything there that she wants, she'll just take it. If the scraps are below grade, she'll do without.

Cats won't run races for people to bet on.

No cat would answer to a dumb name like Fido.

Cats Take Revenge

Steve Sprat thinks he teased his cat once too often, something he agrees a person nearly twenty years old should know not to do. Anyhow, Sprat's cat took her revenge by night. She crawled into bed with him, down under the covers near his knees, and wet the bed. Steve says she wanted to make his mom think that he, not the cat, had wet the bed, and that's why she went under the covers instead of on top of them, the way any reasonable cat would pee on a bed.

Paul, an advertising executive, is a widower who treats his pair of cats, a Siamese and a Manx, very, very well. For dinner he always feeds them special canned gourmet cat dinners, never mind the cost, and he hardly ever leaves them alone for long. It seemed a small thing for him to be gone for two days just this one time. He kept an all-talk radio station turned on for them, left lights burning in the bedroom, and put down amply filled bowls of the best quality dried cat food he could find.

When Paul returned from his trip, he found the cats hadn't eaten more than a bite or two. Instead, they had systematically carried pieces of dried food to every cranny and corner of the apartment, so that the floor in every room was covered with dry cat food. Cleaning up took him several hours. He hasn't gone away since.

They couldn't seem to get the timing right to have Tiger spayed; thus they didn't have the kitty factor under control. After dealing with two unwanted litters, they despaired and took Tiger to an animal shelter about thirty miles away. Three months later, the family came home from work and school to find Tiger stretched out on the older son's bed, purring, of course. You just can't evict a purring cat, so they let her stay. A week or so later, Tiger had kittens. In a few more days, one of Tiger's earlier offspring also had kittens. Everyone cooperated in catching both females at the right moment for spaying, after that, because they were afraid if they took two females to the shelter, two females would find their way back, have kittens, who would go to the shelter, come back to have kittens who would have kittens . . .

Because of the delicate nature of this story, all participants remain anonymous. The characters are Roommate Number One, Roommate Number Two, and Cat. Cat belonged to Roommate Number One, but he chewed up a favorite flowering houseplant of Roommate Number Two, who promptly set him in a corner, told him he was a bad cat, and took away his supper, all while Roommate Number One was gone to work. Cat didn't complain to Roommate Number One when she came home, and Roommate Number Two got engrossed in "L.A. Law" and forgot all about the incident. The roommates watched television together for a while. Cat waited. Finally the girls went to their rooms to get ready for bed. Cat waited. By midnight, both roommates were sound asleep in their respective beds. And then it was that Cat crept in and did a most unseemly thing on the sleeping head of Roommate Number Two, then crept out again.

Everybody lives someplace else now.

Cats Have Devious Ways to Get What They Want

Pauline was an inn cat. By day she roamed the yard, snoozed on the back porch, accepted petting from guests in the lobby, and ate from her special Wedgwood bowl behind the check-in desk. At night she curled up there, behind the desk on her special needlepoint cushion, and slept until breakfast preparations woke her. It all worked perfectly. Until she had kittens.

Pauline refused to be alone with the kittens. During the day, attention from time to time from whoever passed the desk was enough. Come night, Pauline wanted company and she wanted it there at the desk. As soon as the last person left the lobby she started to caterwaul. Her owners left the TV on for her. It worked for about half an hour, then she recognized the con and started yowling louder than ever.

Her owners tried moving the feline family to their own bedroom. Before everyone had finished brushing their teeth, Pauline had moved all five kit-

41

tens back to the desk and was yowling again.

A guest offered to keep Pauline and her babies in his own room. She repaid him by making a puddle in his wingtips. And then she moved the babies back to the desk. Her racket kept everyone awake.

Finally, two sleepless nights later, the human mistress of the inn set up a cot behind the check-in desk, next to the special pillow and young offspring of the true mistess of the inn, and everyone slept peacefully through the night. The arrangement continued until the kittens were big enough to begin devising devious tricks of their own, and were too big for Pauline to carry in her mouth.

Guggle and Zatch are the newest pets in a household that has been matching minds against kitty scams for thirty years. Tig Burnett unfailingly has her new arrivals neutered and spayed at the earliest appropriate moment. Zatch's time had come. Today he was due to visit the vet. Guggle, a glossy black-and-white female, had already made the trip a couple of months before. Zatch must have been desperate to avoid his fate, or to live life to the fullest before it happened, because the night before he attempted a romantic liaison with a skunk. He'd been following Guggle around and chewing on her neck whenever he could corner her, despite her considerable protests. Presumably he then slipped up behind a skunk, decided her charms far exceeded Guggle's, and began to express his ardor. The skunk was sufficiently startled that it didn't load down the atmosphere with its perfume, but it managed to dose Zatch so that he was a very lonesome cat afterwards. Eventually Tig caught him long enough to wash his paws, and by the next day the smell had died down a little, which was helpful for the people who had to perform the operation. It's possible that Zatch got confused and thought the black-and-white skunk was his black-and-white buddy, Guggle, but it seems more likely that the attack on the skunk was a last-ditch attempt by Zatch to preserve his machismo.

Marlow has his routines and he expects them to be honored. One morning, Liz, his keeper, was sick as a dog, excuse the expression, and stayed in bed. Marlow didn't like that and nudged and purred and meowed to rouse Liz, who dug deeper into the covers. Then all of a sudden she heard, not two feet away from the bed, awful gagging and retching sounds. Liz leapt from bed and hastened him downstairs away from the carpet. The instant she put the cat down, he stretched, put his tail straight up, and ambled toward the door. Liz figured it out. "Marlow was not sick. He faked me out just as sure as a Monday-morning schoolboy."

You'd have thought the Homans' cats had everything a cat could want. Well, they didn't have names, because there were so many of them and, mostly, farmers don't give their barn cats names. But these cats had all the fresh, warm, creamy milk they could drink, all the mice they could chase, and all the soft hay they needed to sleep in. What they didn't have was tender loving care. Nobody in a dairy barn has time for petting cats. They took care of it. They started walking up and down the feeding troughs at feeding time. It only took a couple of weeks to train the hundred or so cows. Soon, as the cats walked by, each cow stopped eating long enough to give each passing cat one long lick of the tongue. And so, in command of the world's largest petting machine, the Homans' barn cats lived happily ever after.

Claudette Price's cat, Charlie, doesn't like to be left alone either, not even in the company of his cat mate, Barney. Unless there's a human on the scene, Charlie considers himself alone. When Claudette travels, she enlists a neighbor to come in a couple of times a day to scoop the tuna and salmon goodies into the cats' bowls. Believe it: these cats eat well. Or they did. It's getting harder and harder to coax the neighbor to do the feeding, because Charlie has taken to clutching her around the ankle with both forepaws each time she tries to return home. The only way to get out of that apartment with Charlie holding on is to drag the cat to the door, get most of your leg out, and then try to force Charlie's paws free by closing the door, a little at a time. Claudette hasn't given up travel, because that's what she does to earn money for all the tuna and salmon gourmet dinners the cats eat, but she sure doesn't go anywhere she doesn't have to.

Penny is a Lilac Point Siamese whose approach to feeding is a little different. She doesn't much care who feeds her or whether or not they stick around afterwards, as long as it happens on time. Supper is supposed to be at 6:00 p.m., sharp. If it isn't on time, at 6:03 p.m. Penny starts pushing her feeding bowl across the kitchen floor and keeps it up until food is forthcoming. Penny's keeper replaced the metal bowl with a plastic one, thinking it would make less racket, but it took only one late dinner for Penelope to figure out how to edge the new bowl under a low kitchen shelf and push it back and forth so that it scraped both the floor and the rough underside of the shelf, making more noise than ever. Thus, dinner is at 6:00 p.m., sharp, served in the familiar old metal bowl.

Marthamae will tell you, she doesn't get that many telephone calls from good-looking, charming men, so when her friend Mark calls from Boston for an hour's conversation, it's a big deal. At least it is when Precious, her Seal Point Siamese, is in a good mood. But if Precious doesn't want Marthamae spending a lot of time on the phone, the cat starts screaming into the telephone, biting at the cord, and pulling on Marthamae's clothes until she hangs up. Mark has had some experience with protective fathers, but when it comes to jealous cats, he's new to the game. The end of this story hasn't been written yet.

Tig would rather type her letters than write them out longhand because it goes so much faster, but Higgins doesn't like the clacking sound of the typewriter, so sometimes correspondents receive letters that begin, "I'm sorry not to have written sooner, but Higgie hates the typewriter, and protests loudly when I disturb him with its noise at night. If that doesn't make me stop, he jumps off the desk and stomps away indignantly to a quiet spot in the cellar where he pouts all night." Such letters are always handwritten.

Apparently the cat of Alice Muncaster and Ellen Sawyer has nothing against typewriters, which is good, because they are authors. You do have to wonder, though, about the behavior of the animal that inspired their book titles: *The Cat Made Me Buy It* and *The Cat Sold It.* And the new title, *The Black Cat Made Me Do It,* makes you wonder if the problem is getting better, or worse, or just more specific.

There's Nothing Like a Good Chase

Dot and Norman were named for the kids' grandparents because, like the grandparents, the two cats relied mostly on each other for company, without too much worry for the opinions of the rest of the world. You could hear it in their names. Whoever would go around calling, "Here Norman, here Norman"? And who but the human Norman could have gotten away with fifty years of whistling a little triplet instead of calling Dot's name.

So the behavior of the feline Dot and Norm seemed exactly right to those who knew their namesakes. The two cats spent most of their time chasing one another closely, in movements so synchronized that they seemed to be joined by a short string. The best part of the chase always came in the kitchen, where the cats turned a sharp corner from the hall, then locked their legs to brake, and skidded in unison across the highly waxed floor. One day as they skidded by, Norman noticed a bowl of food that wasn't usually there. He couldn't stop sliding, so he took a swipe at the bowl as he slid past. In perfect synchronization, Dot extended a paw to duplicate the effort to grab the bowl and, being a little closer, she connected. That sent the bowl spinning, the dry food rattling and flying, and ultimately left the two cats, the bowl, and a heap of food racked up against the kitchen wall. No harm done. After collecting themselves for a minute or so, Dot and Norman began munching on the food as if they always ate from a heap strewn along the baseboard. Next day they resumed the chase as if nothing had ever happened.

In this story, Freddy is the cat. Laura is the little girl who has just learned to toddle. She's not too steady, but, boy, is she fast! Freddy didn't have a lot to do until Laura got mobile; now he's endlessly and happily amused. He chases Laura the way other cats chase a ball. When Laura plops down, Freddy pounces (with claws retracted) on a foot or leg to signify fair catch, then sits back to wait for the Laura ball to start rolling again. Laura's first word wasn't "Mama" or "Daddy," it was "Freddy."

Freckles liked to chase squirrels. She single-handedly kept all the squirrels in oak trees out back scared to death most of the time. Her favorite game for almost five years was to find a squirrel digging for acorns on the ground, chase it at high speed across the yard, and follow it up to the first limbs on a tree. Then she'd jump down and saunter away, leaving the squirrel hiding in the treetop. One warm spring afternoon, she began the usual chase, but squirrel sap must have been rising faster than kitty juices that day, because just at the base of the tree, the squirrel turned on Freckles and chased the startled cat all the way to the house, where she leapt to a windowsill, knocked out a screen, and hid inside. Freckles never chased another squirrel that spring or any spring to come.

Cats That Think They're Human
Learn All the Human Vices

Pitty-Pat Cat and her Yuppie family live in Winston-Salem, North Carolina—tobacco country. Pitty-Pat has a pack-a-day habit. Worse yet, being an unemployed feline, she uses OPs, other people's. Quite a few cigarettes get spoiled when Pitty-Pat has to open a new pack herself. If the pack is already open, she holds it against whatever surface it's lying on with one paw and bats the closed end of the pack with the other paw until the tip of a cigarette protrudes from the open end. Then she grasps the cigarette in her mouth, pulls it free of the pack, settles back on her haunches with a sigh, and lets the filthy weed dangle from her mouth. She sits this way for five or ten minutes, gives the cigarette a couple of chews so nobody else will want it, and drops it on the floor. Rumor has it that she experimented with some funny cigarettes a couple of times, too, but her supply dried up and, being limited to OPs, she's confined her filthy habit to tobacco.

The fraternity brothers fed Namath beer in his milk saucer as a joke.

He liked it.

A lot.

Now they're stuck with his demands to set 'em up Joe, because anytime they pour milk into his beer saucer, he steps on the rim, tips it over, and spills the milk on the floor. Currently he's drinking Old Milwaukee. The brothers are forbidden, on pain of expulsion, to introduce him to the expensive imports.

How much television is too much for the average household cat? Experts be damned, Blackie expects three hours a day, starting with early cartoons, followed by *Sesame Street,* and finishing off with *Mr. Rogers.* It was sort of an after-school tradition, especially in winter, for Blackie to sit in the den with Lee and Dana, sharing the popcorn and watching the kids' shows. But that was several years ago. Lee and Dana haven't watched a cartoon or Cookie Monster or the baggy-sweatered Mr. Rogers for a long time because they're too busy tumbling, twirling, practicing for the school play, and working at McDonald's for a few extra bucks. Blackie doesn't care. Every afternoon, come cartoon time, Blackie finds Mommy in the kitchen and starts rubbing against her ankles in a way that the unaware might suppose means Blackie wanted food. Of course Mommy knows better. She turns on TV in the den, and Blackie settles down on the cushion next to where the kids used to sit and attends with perfect concentration until the moment when Mr. Rogers takes off his slippers, puts his shoes back on, and sings "Goodbye, I'm so glad you're my neighbor."

Zabelle Derounian thought about not sharing this story at all, because she was afraid you might think Nutmeg was a deviant cat. She's had Nutmeg for about nine years, during which time she (Nutmeg, that is) always acted perfectly conventional until just five years ago, when she discovered ladies' undies. It started when Zabelle's family, visiting from England, left their suitcases open on the floor while they went off on a picnic. When they returned, they found that Nutmeg had scattered a bikini top, bra, and panty hose across the living room floor. From then on, every time they went out, Nutmeg found the undies and dragged them out again. Zabelle assumed all this kinky behavior would stop as soon as her guests returned to England, taking their bras and bikinis with them.

But a bad habit is hard to shake. Nutmeg simply

made do with bras and panty hose she found on the drying rack. If anything, she's gotten even more kinky. She treats these items like prey, growling, crouching, leaping, and swatting them. She's even become something of an exhibitionist. In the middle of an elegant dinner party, Zabelle said, "Any minute now, Nutmeg will come in with my bra, which she's been stalking." On cue, Nutmeg came in, meowing, dragging a black lace bra.

Whether snobbery is learned or inherited, Curry Mieul had managed to get a good share. She liked the real thing, not cheap imitations—butter, not margarine; cotton, not polyester; wood, not flakeboard; and certainly leather, not vinyl. When the family bought a pretty red vinyl chair to pair with the black leather chair they already had, Curry had a fit. But it was a nice chair. The family ignored Curry's growls and hisses and gave the chair a place of honor by the fireplace. Curry refused to sit in it. Curry refused to stay in the lap of anyone sitting in it. But the family wasn't about to give up a nice chair because of a cat. The red chair stayed by the fireplace. That night Curry made a puddle in it. The family cleaned it up next morning. Before noon, Curry made another puddle in it. The family cleaned it up and shut Curry out of the room. By night, Curry crept back in and made another puddle.

Eventually, the family moved the chair to a basement study, but even there, Curry found the chair and left puddles in it. The family suspected that Curry was having to drink extra water every day to be able to produce the number and volume of puddles with which she filled the red plastic chair.

Of course Curry won. In time the chair smelled so bad they took it to the dump. Curry went back to her normal litterbox habits and never tried to visit the chair at the dump even once.

It was only a matter of time until Mittens got into the tropical fish tank with those big paws. Give a cat seven toes, put her in a house with such colorful, moving temptations, and what do you expect? The first hint of trouble ahead came the day Mittens learned how to flip up the tank's cover. But everyone had been hoping that when it happened, Mittens would settle for scaring a few fish and gloating over it while she licked her seven toes dry. Mittens was obviously a snob too, because it was only the very best for her when the day came. She reached into the tank with all the deftness of a professional aquariast, ignoring the swordtails and danios and gouramis that you can buy for a buck or two. With unerring taste, Mittens went right for the twenty-five-dollar oscar and flipped him out of the tank onto the hardwood floor. The story has a semi-happy ending. Somebody got the oscar back into the tank before it died; from then on Mittens had to limit her living to the back porch and in the kitchen.

A prissy cat is almost as bad as a snobby cat. Aside from her name, there was nothing to make you suspect that Precious was prissy. She was an ordinary calico, raised in a tidy home where manners mattered, but she didn't have a jeweled collar or a great pedigree, or even a fancy pillow. She did have fastidious eating habits. She liked her feeding dish to be perfectly washed and dried before food went into it. She didn't like the rim of the dish to have any specks of food on it, and she liked the floor around her dish to be shiny clean. She really would have preferred to eat with a sterling silver fork, an affectation she had to forgo not only because she couldn't hold the fork, but also because there was no sterling silver in the house. Precious compromised. She ate with her paw. Only with her paw. What she couldn't put into her mouth by paw, she wouldn't eat. Nor would she use both paws. Each dainty bite balanced on her right paw, while her left rested quietly on the floor. When she was done, she turned away from the disgusting sight of a dirty dish, mewed once, softly, to signal that the dish should be taken away, and then meticulously licked her eating paw clean.

Precious never knew Butterball, which is just as well, because they wouldn't have gotten along, even though they looked a lot alike. Butterball's failing was all too human. She liked to eat, and she wasn't at all fussy about how she got her food to her mouth. She wasn't fussy about where she got the food either. In fact, she wasn't even fussy about what the food was. And when she got pregnant, she didn't follow her vet's advice about not gaining a lot of excess weight that she was just going to have to lose later. Once she was pregnant, Butterball would eat anything she could chew and some things she had to swallow whole, ranging from buttered popcorn to blue-tail lizards. She seemed to think that leaving the tails of the lizards and the unpopped kernels of the popcorn constituted some sort of diet and expected to be rewarded for her restraint with a tasty treat.

Shortly before she delivered her litter of kittens, she was so nearly round that she couldn't reach her sides with her hind feet to scratch. Until giving birth and a strict diet relieved her misery, she spent a lot of time scratching, frustrated by the fact that the itch never went away because her scratching foot came a full two inches short of the spot that itched.

Maybe the only food vice more annoying than gluttony is persnickety eating. Even that isn't so bad if one is subtle about it. It's the showboats that get to you.

Persnickety, that's Daniel, Karen Foster's cat; and ostentatious about it, too. Take the night Karen was making burritos. As she cooked, she gave Daniel bits of various foods, a little curl of cheese, a dab of sour cream, and so on, all of which he ate. Then she put a little bit of refried beans on the floor, and he sniffed it, turned around, and started making covering-up motions. A witness to the scene swears the burritos were nonetheless delicious.

Savey Trinca's cat had a thing for food, too. But, like Savey, she was the back-to-nature type, with a clear preference for garden produce, particularly zucchini. An Italian gardener will tolerate practically anything from his pets, but not a cat eating his entire crop of zucchini. The cat's taste for squash persisted to the point where Savey decided the addiction required desperate measures if he meant to save his garden. He assigned a built-in desk in the kitchen just to the cat, laying out a fresh, plump zucchini on a piece of aluminum foil every morning. Being as fond of the easy way as most humans, the cat accepted the daily zucchini enthusiastically and left what grew in the garden alone.

Frisky's problem was obsession. Or maybe it was persistence, in which case it wasn't a vice at all, but a virtue. Then again, it might have been stubbornness, clearly a vice. Frisky's family lived on a lake. Frisky liked to sleep on the motor of their boat when it was docked. He would walk across the railing of the dock, jump across to the boat, climb up onto the motor, curl up, and go to sleep. The trouble was that Frisky's balance wasn't very good when he was sleeping. In short order he would fall off, into the water, and have to swim back to the dock. Then he would walk across the railing, jump from the dock to the boat, climb up onto the motor, curl up, and go to sleep. Until he fell into the water again. And would have to swim back to the dock, walk across the railing, jump to the boat, climb up onto the motor, curl up, and go to sleep. Until . . .

At most recent count, Frisky repeated the process fifteen times in one afternoon. Here's a thought. Maybe he's neither obsessive nor persistent nor stubborn. Maybe he's stupid.

You Can Count on Cats to Go for the Best Deal

In the beginning, the cute little calico kitten was called "Callie." Callie lived with a nice couple in the suburbs, where she enjoyed regular meals of a name brand dried cat food and occasional scraps from the couple's vegetarian dinners. When a new family moved into the house next door, Callie went to call and, upon discovering that they were carnivores all, relocated. Her new owners call her Callie as they slip her scraps of roast beef and steak from their plates. Back in her old home, she's known as Benedict Arnold.

The college students who brought Erma into their condo near campus kept food and water out for her all the time. They wondered why sometimes her food went untouched for two or three days in a row, when other times she ate everything. One evening they noticed when they went next door to study that the students in the next condo space also had cat food and water out, even though they didn't have a cat. A little more investigation showed that no fewer than five apartments kept cat food and water out for the roaming Erma, who traveled from condo to condo by crawling through gaps in the closets where the back wall didn't come all the way to the floor. Seems Erma checked out all the offerings and ate whatever looked to her like the best meal every day. Everyone's waiting for the day she will have to commit to one condo because she's become too fat to crawl under the wall.

Cats in the Media

A southern publisher of fiction says the reason they don't publish cookbooks is that the dog they keep on staff to try all the recipes that are submitted has rejected everything they've tried so far, and they won't publish a book of recipes the taster dog won't eat.

So inspired, a California book publishing company has acquired Shakespeare, a dignified tabby of considerable size to whom they read all the fiction submitted for publication. They won't publish any stories Shakespeare doesn't like. So far he hasn't liked any.

Which reminds us again of Marlow, another publisher's cat, who was doing a little self-directed editorial work one day, and threw up on an unsolicited manuscript. What could the human members of the office staff do but sit down to pen this letter: "Dear Author, We were unable to accept your manuscript in the condition in which we found it . . ."

 65

Another fussy cat went public on a West Coast talk show with his disdain for both publishing and recipes. John Storey's publishing house was working hard to publicize its cookbook for cats—not a book on cooking cats, understand, but one on cooking for cats, a book full of recipes for homemade cat food. John rose from his bed very early of a Vermont morning to hand-carry a Thermos full of choice homemade kitty food prepared from one of the book's recipes to a California television studio, where the producer's own cat was scheduled to sample the delicacy on live TV. John hurried from the airport directly to the studio, clutching his Thermos as seriously as others on the flight carried their briefcases. He made it by air time, told the TV audience about the cat cookbook, and scooped a generous portion of homemade cat food into the feeding bowl on the floor of the set. Then the host let the cat out of the cage. That cat took one sniff of the food, let out a yowl, slammed himself back into the cage, turned his back, and refused to come out again. That was a live review; film at eleven.

Bob, the Weather Cat, a regular performer on KATU-TV's evening weather show in Portland, has been on the air for more than three years. He wears costumes of various professions: nurse, policeman, ballerina, and the like. He started out as an ordinary rescued stray, but once he'd wandered into a video show in his yard, he developed a taste for celebrity life and has been working ever since. Being a smart cat, he doesn't even try to predict weather, just leaves that to the humans. Since he never predicts, he's never wrong. That makes him very, very popular with viewers. So he has collected more than four thousand fan letters, significantly more than the predicting humans get.

According to one of the major scandal sheet tabloids, this tiger cat named "Birdie" ate a parrot and has been going around ever since asking for crackers. We're still checking our sources.

To contribute to future volumes of this book,
send your cat tales to:

Cats
August House Publishers
P.O. Box 3223
Little Rock, AR 72203